my first book of
QUESTIONS AND ANSWERS
about
WINGS
AND
WHEELS

James Pickering

p

This is a Parragon Publishing Book
First published in 2001

Parragon Publishing
Queen Street House
4 Queen Street
Bath BA1 1HE, UK

Produced by

David West ⚇ Children's Books
7 Princeton Court
55 Felsham Road
Putney
London SW15 1AZ, UK

British Library Cataloguing-in-Publication Data

A catalogue record for this book is available from the British Library.

ISBN 0-75255-848-X

Printed in China

Designers
Axis Design, Aarti Parmar, Rob Shone, Fiona Thorne

Illustrators
Colin Howard, Mike Lacey, Dud Moseley, Geoff Pleasance, Terry Riley (SGA)

Cartoonist
Peter Wilks (SGA)

Editor
Ross McLaughness

CONTENTS

WHAT IS A MUSCLE CAR?
and other questions about motor cars

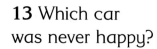

27 What is a muscle car?

28 What was an Aerocar?

28 Which car could dive underwater?

29 What is a hot rod?

30 What is a dragster?

31 What's the fastest car ever?

31 Which bird traveled at 300 mph?

32 Which car could drive itself?

32 What was Chitty Chitty Bang Bang?

33 Which car had an ejector seat?

34 What was Sunraycer?

35 Which car fits in a suitcase?

35 How fast can electric cars travel?

WHICH TRUCKS CRUSH CARS? and other questions about trucks and diggers

38 Were there trucks before engines?

39 Which coach ran on steam?

39 What did steam trucks look like?

40 Which car was a truck?

40 What does "cab over engine" mean?

41 What replaced steam trucks?

42 Which trucks bend in the middle?

42 Which trucks have piggybacks?

43 Which trucks deliver cars?

44 What is a low-loader?

45 Which trucks can travel through water?

45 What are caterpillar tracks?

46 How do trucks stop?

46 What is a jackknife?

47 Why do trucks have so many gears?

48 What is a customized truck?

48 What are tractor tuggers?

49 Which trucks crush cars?

50 What is a road train?

50 Which is the biggest truck?

51 What is a digger?

52 Where do truckers sleep?

52 Where do truckers eat?

53 How do truckers talk to each other?

54 Which small trucks carry heavy loads?

54 Which trucks carry logs?

55 Do trucks pull airplanes?

56 Which trucks are freezing?

56 How is gas delivered?

57 What is a container truck?

58 Which truck eats trash?

59 What is a wrecker?

59 Which trucks mix cement?

60 Which trucks are hospitals?

60 Which truck puts out fires?

61 Which trucks are safe?

62 Which trucks travel through the desert?

62 Are there truck races?

63 Can you race a pickup?

64 What is a bulldozer?

64 Which digger does lots of jobs?

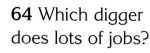

65 What is a mobile crane?

WHAT IS A STUNT PLANE? and other questions about flying machines

68 Who flew the first kites?

68 Who was the first person to fly?

69 What are gliders?

70 Which plane ran on steam power?

70 Who were the Wright brothers?

71 What is a biplane?

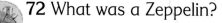

72 What was a Zeppelin?

72 Who flew in a steam powered airship?

73 Do people still fly airships?

74 What was a Blériot?

74 Who were the first to fly across the Atlantic Ocean?

75 Who were the first to fly across the Pacific Ocean?

76 Which planes have floats?

76 What is a flying boat?

77 Which planes can only fly very low?

78 Who flew a Meteor?

78 Who cut through the air with a Sabre?

79 What was a Comet?

80 Who first flew faster than sound?

80 Which plane is a Blackbird?

81 What is a rocket plane?

82 What is a delta wing?

82 Which plane had no wings?

83 Which plane has back-to-front wings?

84 What is a stunt plane?

84 Are there plane races?

85 Where can I see stunt planes?

86 How far can airliners travel?

86 What is the fastest airliner?

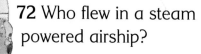

87 Can planes land in cities?

88 Which type of aircraft hovers?

88 What is an air ambulance?

89 Which plane is also a helicopter?

90 What is a rocket belt?

90 What is a jump-jet?

91 Which plane can swivel its engines?

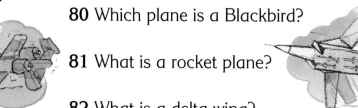

92 What is a hang-glider?

92 What is a microlight?

93 What is a paraglider?

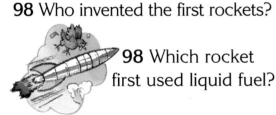

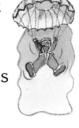
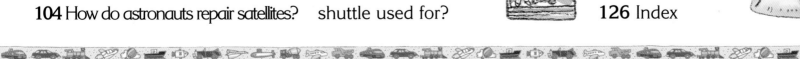

What is a muscle car?

and other questions about motor cars

How did people travel before cars?

Before cars were invented, people often traveled in wheeled carriages, pulled by teams of horses. The journey was dusty, uncomfortable and usually quite slow.

Early steam car

Did cars run on steam?

Several early cars ran on steam power, just like steam trains. Steam engines were more powerful than gasoline engines, but they were very heavy and it was hard work to keep them running.

? *What fuel do cars use?*

For over 100 years, most cars have run on gasoline. At first there were very few gas stations, so most drivers carried cans of spare fuel with them. Cars with gas engines run more quickly than cars with steam engines.

Early petrol station

What was the first car?

The first car to be sold was the three-wheeled Benz Patent Motorwagen, in 1887. It looked more like a chair on wheels than a car, and was so slow that it couldn't travel up hills!

Benz Patent Motorwagen

How were early cars steered?

Early cars didn't have steering wheels. Instead, drivers steered with a lever, or by turning handles on a small wheel at the end of a pole.

?*Who was Daimler?*

Gottlieb Daimler was a German engineer, who built the first ever motorcycle in 1885. He also built one of the first four-wheeled gas driven cars. Daimler's cars were very difficult to drive, but they worked much better than other early cars.

Daimler's first car

? When was the first car race?

The first car race was in 1894, between Paris and Rouen in France – 13 cars took part. The fastest was a huge de Dion steam tractor, which traveled at less than 12 mph.

Early car race

? *What was a "Blower Bentley?"*

"Blower Bentleys" were very fast racing cars in the 1920s and 1930s. They were fitted with a blower, or supercharger, which drove extra fuel into the engine to make the car super-quick.

Blower Bentley

? *Which car was never happy?*

Camille Jenatzy's electric car was called "La Jamais Contente," ("never happy" in French). But Jenatzy was happy, when the car broke the world speed record.

"La Jamais Contente"

TRUE OR FALSE?

Car races were dangerous.

TRUE. Early cars had very bad brakes, and often had accidents. Drivers weren't protected by helmets or seat belts, and races took place on public roads, crowded with spectators.

Rocket cars were invented long before space rockets.

TRUE. The Heylandt rocket car was first driven in 1931. The first space rocket flew 26 years later.

? Which car was a baby?

The Austin Seven was nicknamed the "baby Austin" because it was so tiny. Four people could only just fit inside it, but it became Britain's most popular car in the 1920s.

Austin Seven

? Which cars only came in black?

The Model "T" Ford, or "Tin Lizzie," always left the factory painted black. In its day, the Model "T" was the most popular car in the world. Over 15 million were built!

Model "T" Ford

Charabanc

Fords moved along a line.

TRUE. Fords were the first cars to be built on a moving line. Parts were added until the cars were finished at the end of the line.

All cars had hard roofs.

FALSE. Early cars had soft roofs which folded down. Motorists baked in the summer, and froze in the winter!

❓ Which car traveled to the beach?

Charabancs were the first motorized coaches. Groups of friends used to hire long charabancs for special trips to the beach or to the city. The passengers sat on wooden benches behind the driver.

? *Which car was the most comfortable?*

Rolls Royces are very quiet, comfortable and expensive cars. The 1907 Silver Ghost was no exception. Owners rarely drove themselves, but preferred to relax in the back!

Rolls Royce Silver Ghost

? *Which car was "royal?"*

Ettore Bugatti hoped that every royal family in Europe would buy a Bugatti Royale, but only six were ever built. Today, each one is worth millions of dollars.

Bugatti Royale

? *What was a Cord?*

The Cord was one of the most comfortable American cars of the 1920s and 1930s, but they were very expensive, and very few were built. Luckily, many of them still exist.

Cord 810

TRUE OR FALSE?

Passengers could eat a picnic in the car.

TRUE. Luxury cars, such as Rolls Royces, had picnic tables in the back, which folded down if passengers ever got hungry!

All cars had electric horns.

FALSE. Early motorists had to squeeze the horns on their cars, to warn other drivers. Horns on modern cars are powered by electricity.

? Who built big family cars?

American cars were always much bigger than European cars. The roads were wider, and gas was also cheaper than in Europe, which meant that many American families could afford to run a large family car.

1939 Plymouth

? What is a "Beetle?"

The first Volkswagen was nicknamed the "Beetle" or "Bug" because it looks a bit like an insect. Over 40 million have been made since 1938.

? *Where was the first freeway?*

Before cars were invented, most roads were narrow and bumpy. As cars became faster, bigger roads were needed. The first freeway was built in Germany in 1921.

Volkswagen Beetles

TRUE OR FALSE?

Beetles are able to swim.

TRUE. During World War Two, the German army built a special Volkswagen Beetle, which could travel through rivers.

Motorists often lost their way.

TRUE. There used to be very few road signs, so it was difficult to find your way. Sensible motorists carried maps in their cars.

What is a rally car?

Rally cars are family cars, which have been given extra-powerful engines for off-road racing. Rally cars skid across country, through mud, snow and across ice. Accidents often happen, and drivers are protected by crash helmets and safety harnesses.

What is Formula One?

Formula One racing takes place around the world every year. Formula One cars have very powerful engines and huge fins, which stop the cars from taking off at high speed!

Formula One racing car

Rally car

? *How fast can racing cars go?*

Formula One cars race at speeds of over 150 mph, but American Indycar racing is faster. Indycars can zoom along at 230 mph – that's over four times faster than the speed limit on American freeways.

Indycar racer

❓ Which cars had fins?

Oldsmobile

During the 1950s, many colorful American cars, such as Oldsmobiles, had huge fins, shiny metal bumpers and bright lights fitted to them. Some of them looked more like alien spaceships than cars!

❓ Which cars are stretched?

Stretched limousine

Limousines can be stretched, so that they are as long as a train. The longest limousine in the world had 26 wheels, a swimming pool, a bed and a helicopter landing pad! It was 100 feet long – about ten times longer than a family car.

Tucker '48

? Which car was a goose?

The Tucker '48 was an unusual car, nicknamed the "Tin Goose." The engine was at the back of the car, and its front headlight swiveled as the driver turned the steering wheel.

Who traveled in a bubble?

The BMW Isetta was nicknamed the "bubble car" because of its shape. These tiny three-wheelers only had one door, at the front. There was only room for the driver and one passenger.

BMW Isetta "bubble car"

Which car is smart?

The Smart Car is a very small modern car which is perfect for zipping around crowded cities. Because it's so short and slim, the Smart Car takes up very little room when it's not being used – drivers can park it sideways against the sidewalk.

Smart Car

Renault Zoom concept car

Frogeyes look like frogs.

TRUE. The Austin Healey Sprite was nicknamed the Frogeye, because its big headlights and radiator grill make it look like a cheeky, smiling frog!

❓*Which car can fold up?*

The Renault Zoom can fold up its back wheels to make itself shorter, so that it can park in small spaces. It also has an electric motor, instead of a gas engine, and doesn't make lots of dirty fumes like other cars.

You can race in a Mini.

TRUE. Minis won the Monte Carlo rally three times. They were good rally cars, partly because they could be steered around corners very quickly.

❓ *What is a sports car?*

Ferrari F40

Sports cars are meant to be driven for fun. Often they have a fold-down roof, a small trunk, and they're usually much faster than ordinary cars.

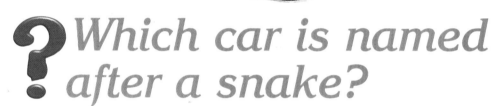

❓ *Which car is named after a snake?*

The AC Cobra is named after a poisonous snake. These cars have massive engines, fat tires and extra-strong bodies for driving at high speed. Cobras make superb racing cars.

AC Cobra

❓ *What is a muscle car?*

Muscle cars are ordinary cars which have been souped-up for high performance. The Shelby Mustang was a Ford Mustang, specially tuned by racing driver Carroll Shelby.

Shelby Mustang

? What was an Aerocar?

The Aerocar was a car which could really fly. When it was driving on the road, the Aerocar folded up its wings and tail.

Aerocar

? Which car could dive underwater?

In the film The Spy Who Loved Me, James Bond's Lotus sports car could turn into a submarine and swim underwater. People got a shock when they saw it driving out of the water on to a beach!

James Bond's Lotus Esprit

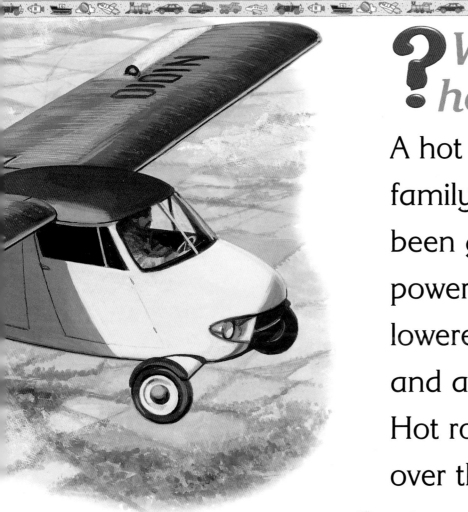

? *What is a hot rod?*

A hot rod is an old family car which has been given an extra-powerful engine, a lowered roof, huge tires and a colorful paint job. Hot rods are raced all over the world.

Hot rods

? *What is a dragster?*

A dragster is a very powerful racing car, which races along a short track at enormous speed. Dragsters are so fast that brakes alone can't stop them – they also need parachutes to slow them down.

Thrust SSC

Dragster

? *What's the fastest car ever?*

Thrust SSC was the first car to travel faster than the speed of sound, in 1997. Thrust had four parachutes and two massive jet engines, which are normally used to power fighter aircraft!

Bluebird

? *Which bird traveled at 300 mph?*

Malcolm Campbell broke the land speed record nine times in his Bluebird cars during the 1930s. 300 mph is about twice as fast as a modern sports car can travel.

? Which car could drive itself?

KITT was the name of a special car in the television series Knightrider. KITT could drive on its own, and could even talk to its owner, to warn him if he was being followed by villains!

KITT

Chitty Chitty Bang Bang

? What was Chitty Chitty Bang Bang?

Only three Chitty Chitty Bang Bang cars were built. They had huge, powerful plane engines, and won many races, even though they were difficult to drive and hardly had any brakes.

? *Which car had an ejector seat?*

James Bond's Aston Martin DB5 had an ejector seat. When he wanted to get rid of someone, Bond pressed a button, the roof opened, and his passenger was shot into the air!

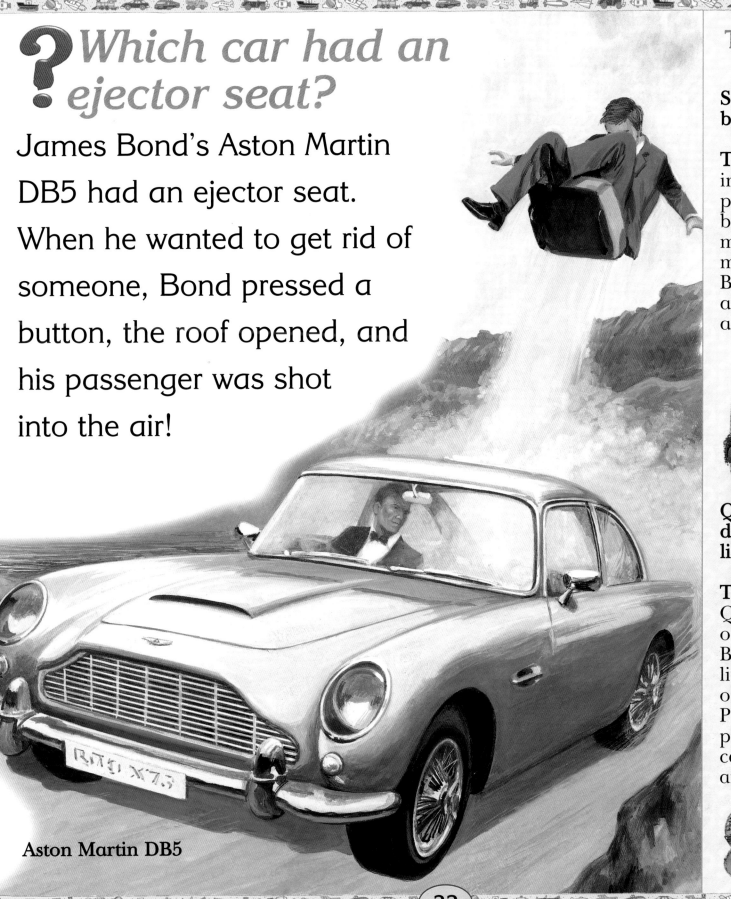

Aston Martin DB5

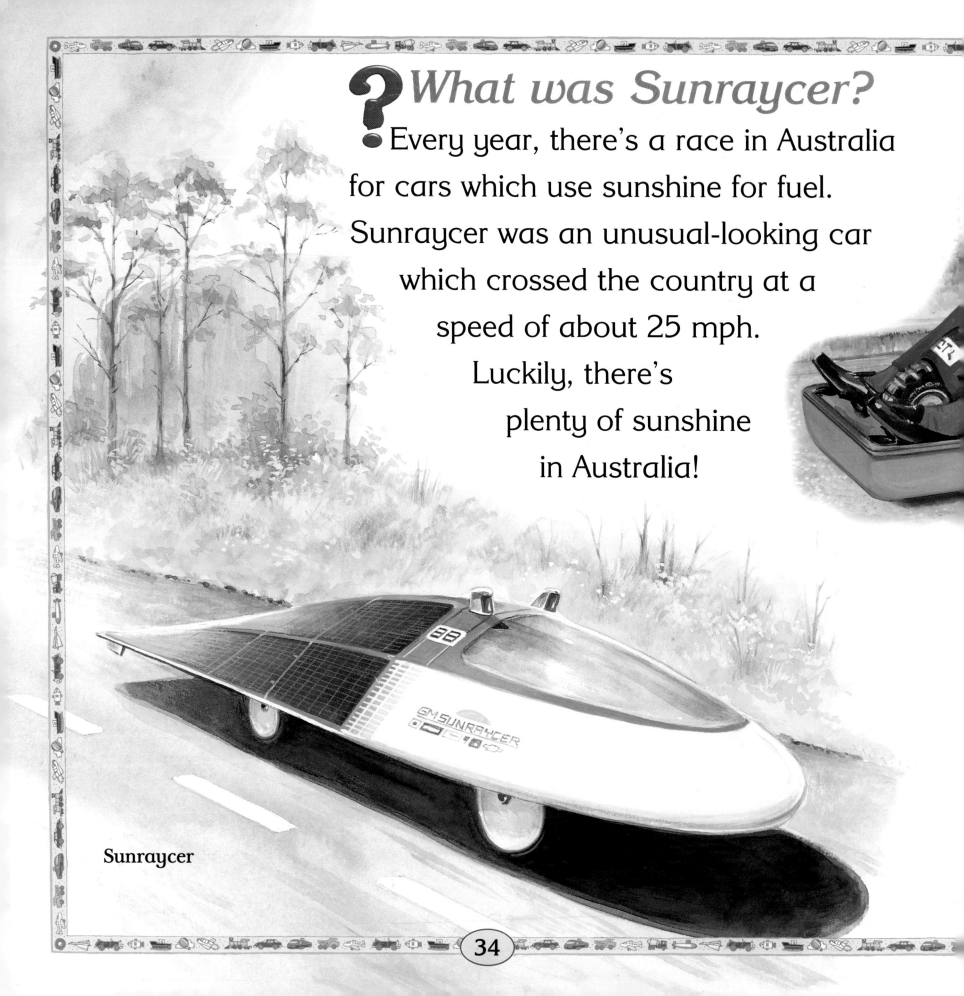

❓ *What was Sunraycer?*

Every year, there's a race in Australia for cars which use sunshine for fuel. Sunraycer was an unusual-looking car which crossed the country at a speed of about 25 mph.

Luckily, there's plenty of sunshine in Australia!

Sunraycer

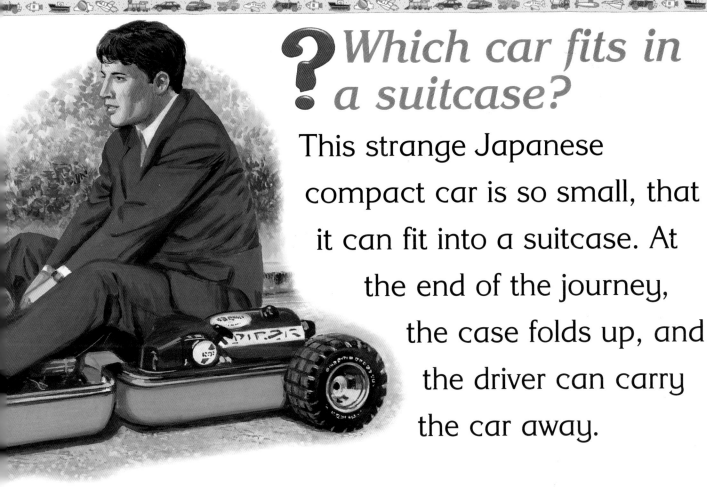

? Which car fits in a suitcase?

This strange Japanese compact car is so small, that it can fit into a suitcase. At the end of the journey, the case folds up, and the driver can carry the car away.

? How fast can electric cars travel?

Electric cars are usually slower than gas-driven cars, but one electric three-wheeler called Alien was said to have reached 150 mph – as fast as a modern sports car.

Alien

Which trucks crush cars?

and other questions about trucks and diggers

Dray-horses and cart

Steam truck

❓ *Were there trucks before engines?*

Before engines were invented, heavy loads were pulled on carts by teams of large dray-horses. Strong dray-horses were also used to pull plows on farms before motorized tractors were invented.

Which coach ran on steam?

Dr Church's steam coach was built in England in 1833. Up to 50 passengers rode on it, on long journeys between cities. It must have been very noisy and uncomfortable.

Dr Church's steam coach

What did steam trucks look like?

Steam trucks looked like steam trains, with large engines, big iron wheels and smoky funnels. They were so big and heavy that they ruined the roads.

TRUE OR FALSE?

Early trucks were huge.

FALSE. Steam trucks were the largest vehicles on the road, but they were still much smaller than modern trucks.

Steam trucks were very slow.

TRUE. In England, someone had to walk in front of the first trucks, with a red flag to warn other road-users.

Model "T" Ford truck

Which car was a truck?

Many early trucks were really cars which had been given extra parts and made stronger, to carry heavy loads. This 1919 truck was based on the popular Model "T" Ford car.

What does "cab-over-engine" mean?

A cab-over-engine truck is a truck where the driver's cab is on top of the engine. When the engine needs to be repaired, the whole cab tips forward to give the mechanic a good look.

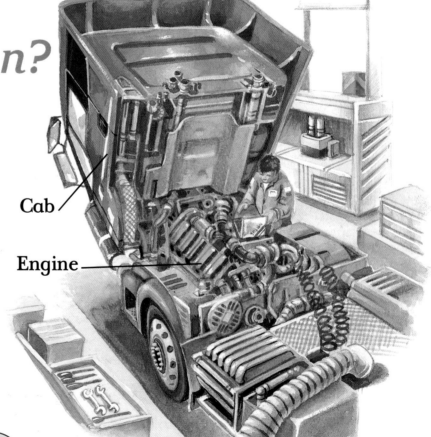

Cab

Engine

? *What replaced steam trucks?*

Steam trucks were noisy, dirty and not very reliable. Gasoline-powered trucks first appeared in 1896, and were much more popular. These days, most trucks run on diesel fuel.

Dennis

Which trucks bend in the middle?

Long articulated trucks, which pull separate trailers, bend in the middle – if they didn't, they wouldn't be able to turn round sharp corners. Shorter trucks, which are built in one piece and don't bend in the middle, are called rigid trucks.

Articulated truck

Which trucks have piggybacks?

New trucks are sometimes delivered by being towed behind another truck, like a trailer. This means that there's less wear on the new trucks' tires, less fuel is burned and only one driver is needed to move several trucks.

? *Which trucks deliver cars?*

Transporters can deliver up to ten cars at a time. The cars are driven on to the transporter up ramps, and they're very carefully strapped down during the journey, so they don't roll off!

Transporter

Piggyback trucks

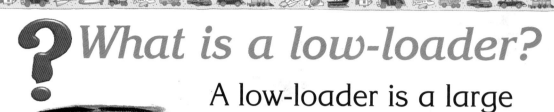

What is a low-loader?

Low-loader

A low-loader is a large transporter truck with a low trailer at the rear. Other vehicles, such as cars, tractors and even tanks, are driven up its ramps and on to the trailer.

Half-track army truck

Caterpillar track

Which trucks can travel through water?

Amphibious truck

Special army trucks, called amphibious trucks, can travel on land and through shallow rivers. The underside of the truck is tightly sealed so that water can't flood into the cab or into the engine.

What are caterpillar tracks?

Caterpillar tracks are knobby strips of metal or rubber, which wrap around the wheels of tanks, bulldozers and other off-road vehicles. They stop the wheels from getting stuck in muddy or sandy ground.

Air-lines

❓ How do trucks stop?

Trucks use air-brakes to stop. An air compressor in the truck sucks in air and squashes it. When the driver presses the brake pedal, the squashed air travels along coiled air-lines and pushes brake shoes against the wheels, slowing them down.

❓ What is a jackknife?

A jackknife is a dangerous accident where a truck slows down, but its trailer slides sideways out of control, sometimes spilling its load on to the road. A jackknife is named after a knife with a folding blade.

This transporter has jackknifed.

❓ *Why do trucks have so many gears?*

Trucks sometimes have over 15 gears, compared to only five or six in a car. Heavy trucks need plenty of low gears to go up and down steep hills, and higher gears to cruise along the open road.

TRUE OR FALSE?

Trucks aren't able to climb steep hills.

FALSE. Trucks can climb hills, but because they're much heavier than cars, they can't do it very quickly!

Truckers need to rest.

TRUE. Truck drivers have to take regular breaks in case they get sleepy at the wheel and cause an accident.

❓*What is a customized truck?*

Truckers often want their trucks to look different from everyone else's. They can customize their trucks by painting them with bright patterns and colors, or by adding extra lights or shiny metal bodywork.

Customized truck

Tractor tugger

❓*What are tractor tuggers?*

Tractor tuggers are powered by fiery aircraft engines! They have to pull a load of 100 tons (as heavy as 100 family cars) for 110 yards in special competitions.

❓ *Which trucks crush cars?*

Monster trucks are small pickup trucks, which have been fitted with enormous dump truck wheels. They take part in races, and drive over large obstacles, including cars, crushing them as flat as pancakes!

Monster truck

? What is a road train?

A road train is a very strong truck, which pulls not one, but several long trailers. Road trains make very long journeys in big countries, such as Australia.

Road train

? Which is the biggest truck?

The biggest truck in the world is a dump truck called the Terex Titan. Each of its wheels is twice as high as a person, and weighs as much as three family cars!

Terex Titan

❓ *What is a digger?*

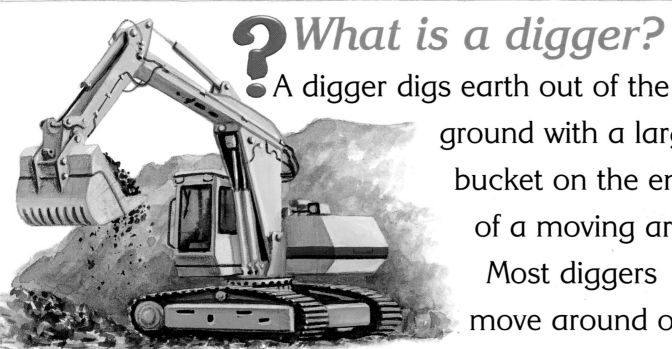

A digger digs earth out of the ground with a large bucket on the end of a moving arm. Most diggers move around on caterpillar tracks.

Digger

TRUE OR FALSE?

Terex Titan travels on the road.

FALSE. Terex Titan is too big to travel on the road. Instead it's taken to pieces, and each part is carried on a transporter.

Some trucks need help from the police.

TRUE. Trucks pulling very large loads need the police to travel with them, to warn other drivers to get out of the way.

Where do truckers sleep?

Truckers are often on the road for several days at a time, and need somewhere to sleep away from home. Some truckers sleep in their cabs, in a bed behind the seats.

Where do truckers eat?

There are truck stops on highways all over the world, where truckers can get a bite to eat, fill up with fuel, wash their clothes, and sometimes even have their hair cut!

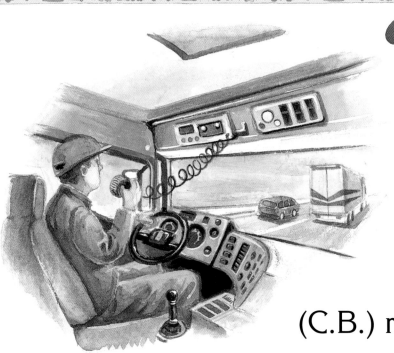

? *How do truckers talk to each other?*

Truckers talk to each other on the move using citizens' band (C.B.) radio. Every trucker has a nickname, and can warn other drivers of hazards, such as traffic jams or bad weather.

Truck stop

TRUE OR FALSE?

Trucks are scrubbed clean.

TRUE. Most truck stops have a drive-through truck wash, where trucks are scrubbed clean with huge soapy brushes.

Trucks never break down.

FALSE. Trucks do break down sometimes. There are usually teams of mechanics and plenty of spare parts at truck stops.

Forklift trucks

❓ Which small trucks carry heavy loads?

Forklift trucks can carry heavy loads around factories, on wooden platforms called pallets. The driver slides the forks underneath the pallets, lifts them into the air, and moves them to another part of the factory.

❓ Which trucks carry logs?

Loggers are large trucks, which carry logs from forests to factories. Logs are much too heavy to be put on a truck by hand, so a logger has its own crane that picks up the logs and puts them on the back of the truck.

❓ *Do trucks pull airplanes?*

● Airport tugs are strong enough to pull large airplanes. These short trucks fit under an airplane's nose, and fix on to its front wheel.

Airport tug

Logger

Freezer truck

? Which trucks are freezing?

A freezer truck is like a big fridge on wheels. It's used to transport food, such as ice cream, which has to stay cold in case it melts.

? How is gas delivered?

Gas is delivered to gas stations in tankers. A tanker can carry enough gas to fill up about 500 family cars. The gas is pumped into a large tank, buried beneath the station.

Gas tanker

Container truck

❓ *What is a container truck?*

Many of the goods you see in stores are made overseas, and arrive on ships in metal boxes called containers. The containers are lifted off the ships and put on to large container trucks, which drive them straight to the stores.

TRUE OR FALSE?

Some trucks tip up.

TRUE. A tipper truck has a special lifting body, which tips up, so that its load simply slides out of the back.

You can fly in a truck.

FALSE. But cherry pickers lift people into the air on a long arm, to do jobs such as changing bulbs in street lamps.

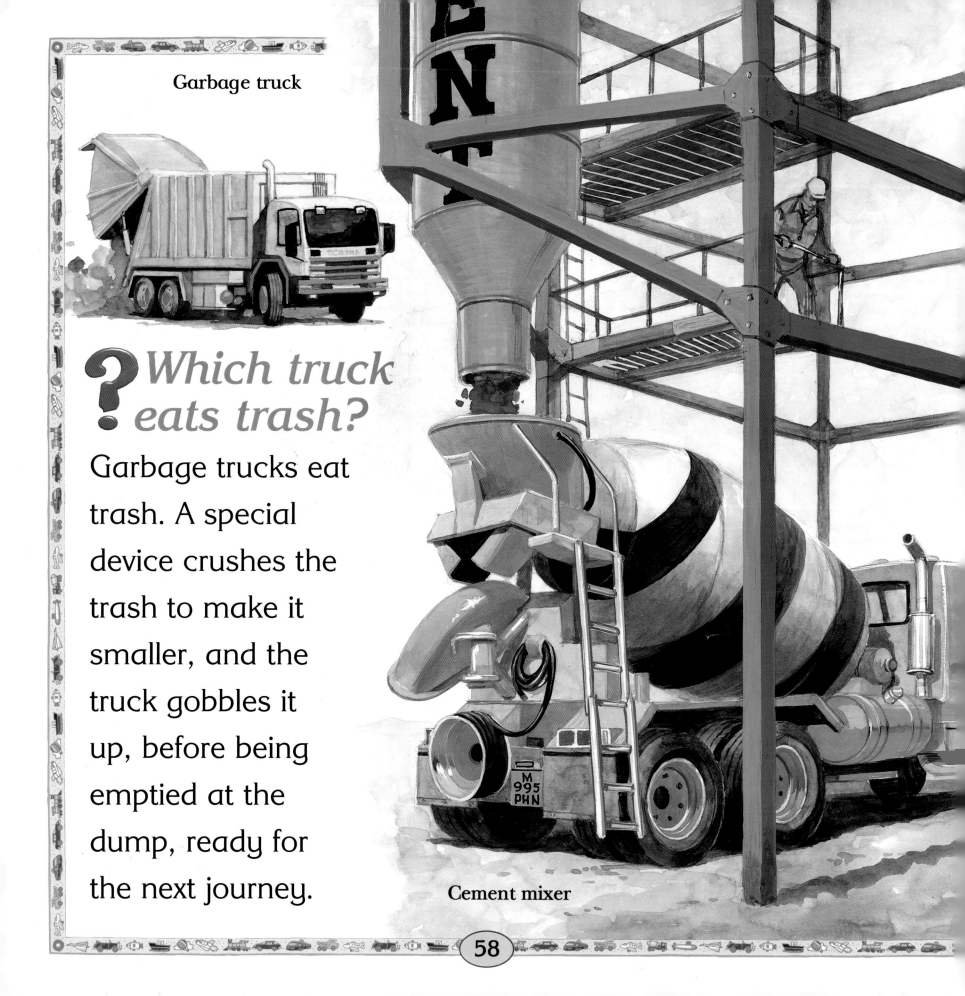

Garbage truck

? Which truck eats trash?

Garbage trucks eat trash. A special device crushes the trash to make it smaller, and the truck gobbles it up, before being emptied at the dump, ready for the next journey.

Cement mixer

? What is a wrecker?

"Wrecker" is the name for a large North American breakdown truck, which can tow away other trucks or cars, if they've broken down or had an accident.

Wrecker

? Which trucks mix cement?

Cement and other ingredients are mixed together in a cement mixer, to make concrete, which is used to make buildings. The ingredients are put in the mixer's drum, which spins around. When the concrete is ready, it's poured out of the cement mixer.

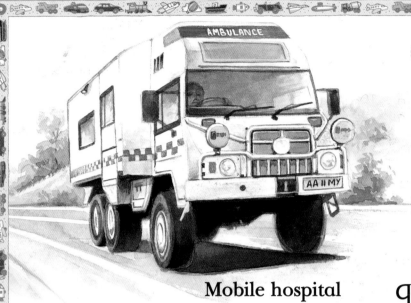
Mobile hospital

❓ Which trucks are hospitals?

An ambulance is a small truck full of emergency equipment, which takes ill people to hospital quickly. But in areas where there are no hospitals, doctors and nurses treat patients in larger trucks called mobile hospitals, where they can even perform life-saving operations.

❓ Which truck puts out fires?

Fire trucks are packed full of equipment to put out fires. They have powerful hoses, medical equipment, axes for breaking down doors, and ladders to reach fires in tall buildings.

Which trucks are safe?

Armor-plated security vans collect money from shops and banks. It's important that the money isn't stolen, so it's kept in a safe, which even the van driver can't open.

Security van

Fire truck

All fire trucks have one driver.

FALSE. Fire trucks with very long ladders, have a second driver who sits on the ladder, steering it safely around corners.

Some fire trucks squirt foam.

TRUE. It's very dangerous to squirt water at fires caused by electricity. Firefighters put out electrical fires with foam instead.

Which trucks travel through the desert?

The Paris-Dakar rally is a very long race for cars and motorcycles through the dusty Sahara desert. Back-up trucks come along too, full of spare parts, in case any of the racers crashes or breaks down.

Paris-Dakar back-up truck

Are there truck races?

You can race almost anything on wheels, including trucks. There are bumpy cross-country rallies, and races around tracks. Some racing trucks are even powered by huge jet engines, and can whiz along more quickly than an express train!

Racing trucks

Pickup racer

? Can you race a pickup?

Pickup trucks are small trucks, which are normally used for carrying small loads, but they can also be raced. Souped-up versions, with low bodies, streamlined shapes and extra-powerful engines race around circuits in America.

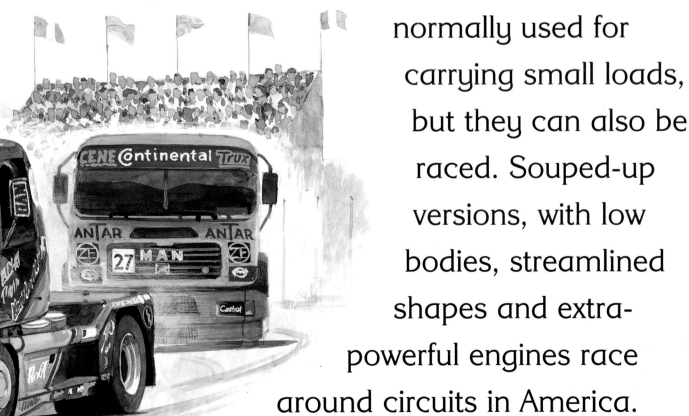

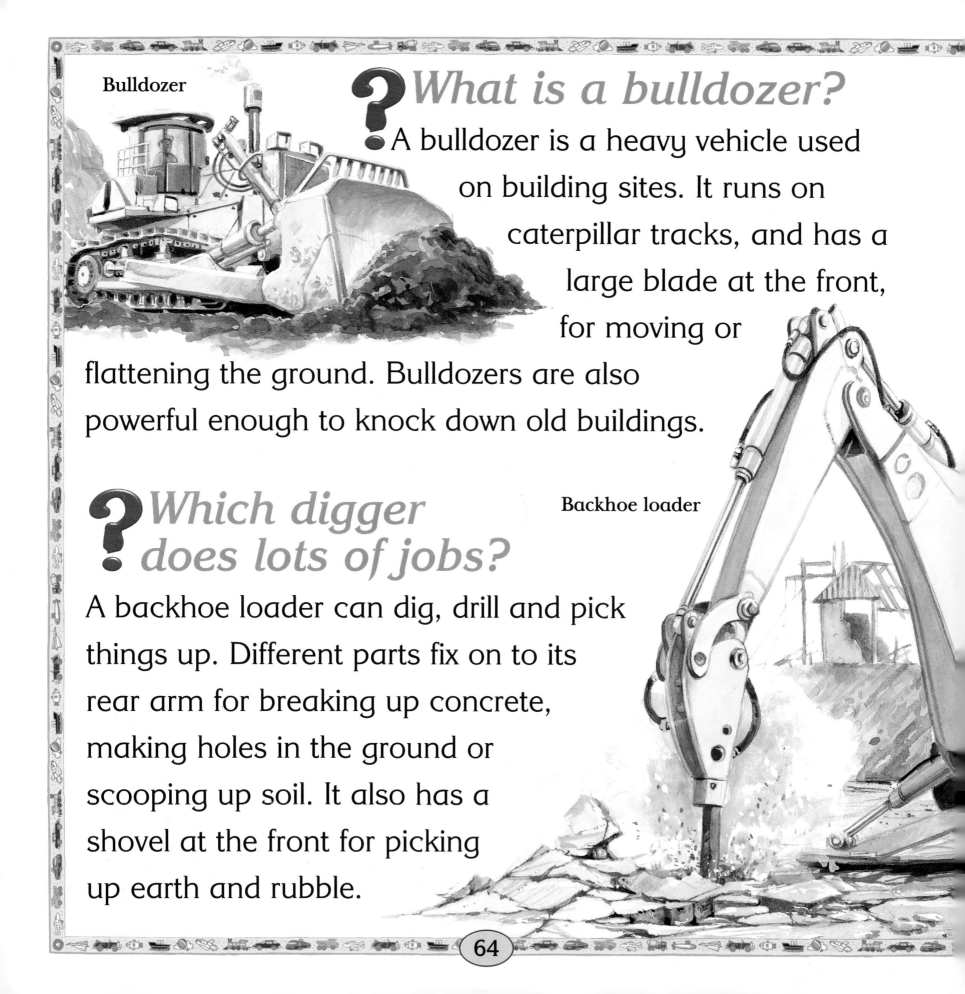

Bulldozer

❓ *What is a bulldozer?*

A bulldozer is a heavy vehicle used on building sites. It runs on caterpillar tracks, and has a large blade at the front, for moving or flattening the ground. Bulldozers are also powerful enough to knock down old buildings.

❓ *Which digger does lots of jobs?*

Backhoe loader

A backhoe loader can dig, drill and pick things up. Different parts fix on to its rear arm for breaking up concrete, making holes in the ground or scooping up soil. It also has a shovel at the front for picking up earth and rubble.

❓ *What is a mobile crane?*

A mobile crane is part truck and part crane. It can be driven on to building sites, where the driver operates the crane from a cab at the back, lifting heavy loads of concrete or metal.

Mobile crane

TRUE OR FALSE?

Diggers have corkscrews.

TRUE. Backhoe loaders often have corkscrew-shaped drills, but they're used for boring holes, not for opening bottles!

Some diggers have hammers.

TRUE. Some diggers have powerful, noisy hammers, called pile drivers, that bang large fence-posts into the ground.

What is a stunt plane?

and other questions about flying machines

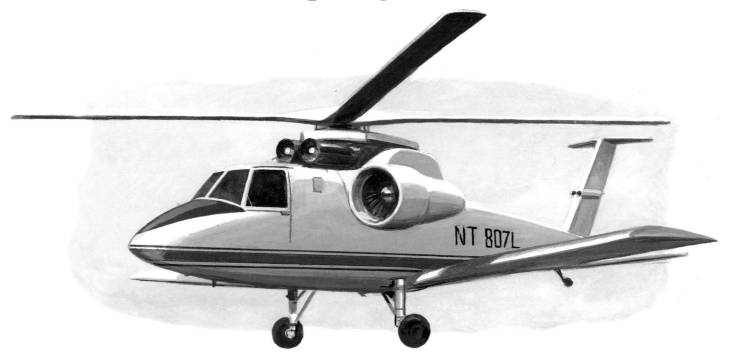

? Who flew the first kites?

The Chinese used to fly kites hundreds of years ago to see if there was enough wind for them to set sail in their ships.

Montgolfière balloon

? Who was the first person to fly?

François Pilâtre de Rozier and the Marquis d'Arlandes flew a Montgolfière balloon in 1783. They traveled 5 miles over Paris, at a height of 2,950 feet.

? *What are gliders?*

Gliders are flying machines without engines. Otto Lilienthal built lots of gliders over 100 years ago. He used to fly them by hanging from a bar under the wings. Sadly, he was killed in a glider crash in 1896.

Otto
Lilienthal

? Which plane ran on steam power?

The odd-looking Eole was flown a short way by Clément Ader in 1890. This steam-powered plane only managed to fly about 8 inches above the ground.

Eole

? Who were the Wright brothers?

Wilbur and Orville Wright were American bicycle makers, who built the first successful airplane with an engine. Orville flew the Flyer for twelve seconds in 1903.

Flyer

❓ *What is a biplane?*

❓A biplane is a small airplane, such as the Sopwith Camel, with two pairs of wings, one above the other. Most early planes were biplanes, and they are still used today for stunt flying.

Sopwith Camel

What was a Zeppelin?

A Zeppelin was a type of airship which flew during the early 20th century. It was filled with hydrogen gas and the passengers traveled in a very comfortable area under the main body of the airship.

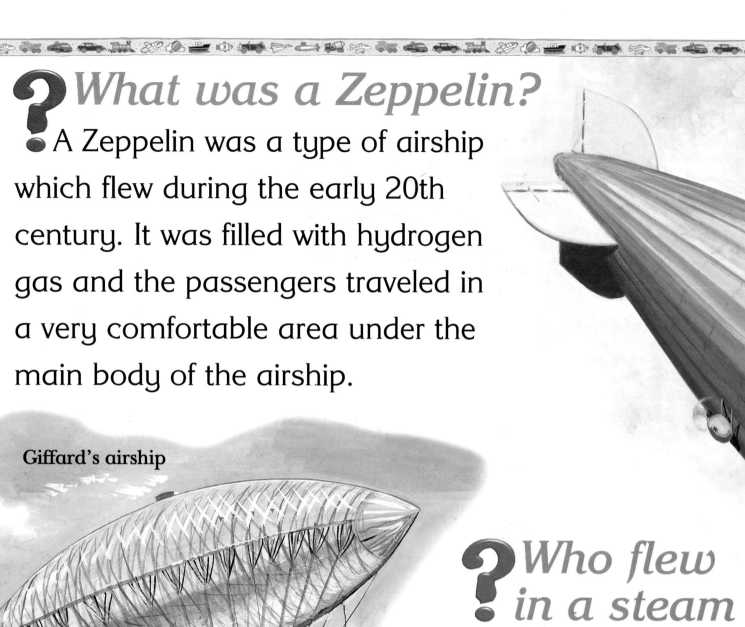

Giffard's airship

Who flew in a steam powered airship?

In 1852, Henri Giffard flew the very first airship, which had a small steam engine and a propeller. It was a slow journey. His airship could only travel at 5 mph.

Modern airship

?Do people still fly airships?

People still fly airships in many parts of the world, but they don't usually carry passengers these days. Airships often carry television cameras to film sports events from the sky.

Graf Zeppelin

Airships are very large.

TRUE. The largest airships were over twice as long as a football field, and much larger than the biggest airplanes.

Airships can only make short journeys.

FALSE. Airships used to fly all the way from Europe to America. The journey took about two days.

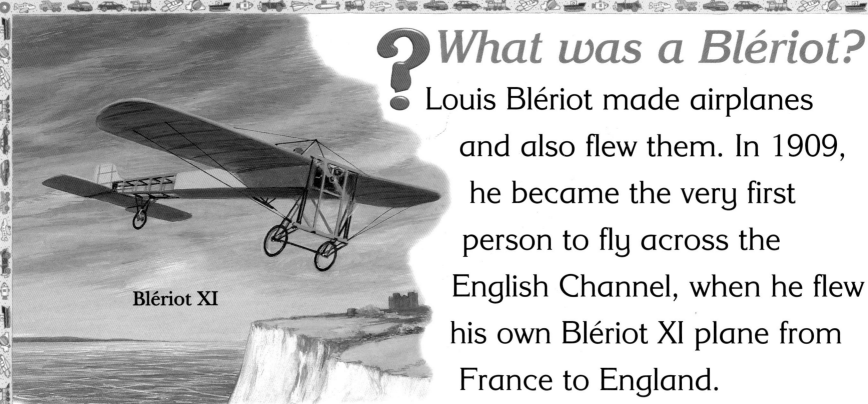

? What was a Blériot?

Louis Blériot made airplanes and also flew them. In 1909, he became the very first person to fly across the English Channel, when he flew his own Blériot XI plane from France to England.

Blériot XI

? Who were the first to fly across the Atlantic Ocean?

The first non-stop flight across the Atlantic was by John Alcock and Arthur Brown in 1919. Their Vickers Vimy plane crash-landed at the end of the flight, but luckily they escaped unhurt.

Vickers Vimy

Southern Cross

? *Who were the first to fly across the Pacific Ocean?*

Charles Kingsford Smith, Charles Ulm and their crew made the first flight across the Pacific in 1928, in their plane Southern Cross. They nearly crashed the plane into some trees when they landed on a small island during the journey.

TRUE OR FALSE?

You can fly on a moth.

TRUE. Amy Johnson was the first person to fly alone from England to Australia in a biplane called a Gypsy Moth.

Lindbergh fell asleep at the controls.

TRUE. Charles Lindbergh took over 33 hours to fly across the Atlantic Ocean. No wonder he nodded off a few times!

Supermarine S 6B seaplane

? Which planes have floats?

Seaplanes have floats instead of wheels, so that they can take off and land on water, using the sea as a runway.

? What is a flying boat?

A flying boat is an airplane which has a body shaped like a large boat. Its wings are attached to the top of the plane, so that it can take off and land safely on water.

G-.AD

? *Which planes can only fly very low?*

Surface-effect vehicles are special planes which only fly a few feet above the surface of the water. Their tiny wings won't allow them to rise high into the air.

Surface-effect vehicle

Canopus flying boat

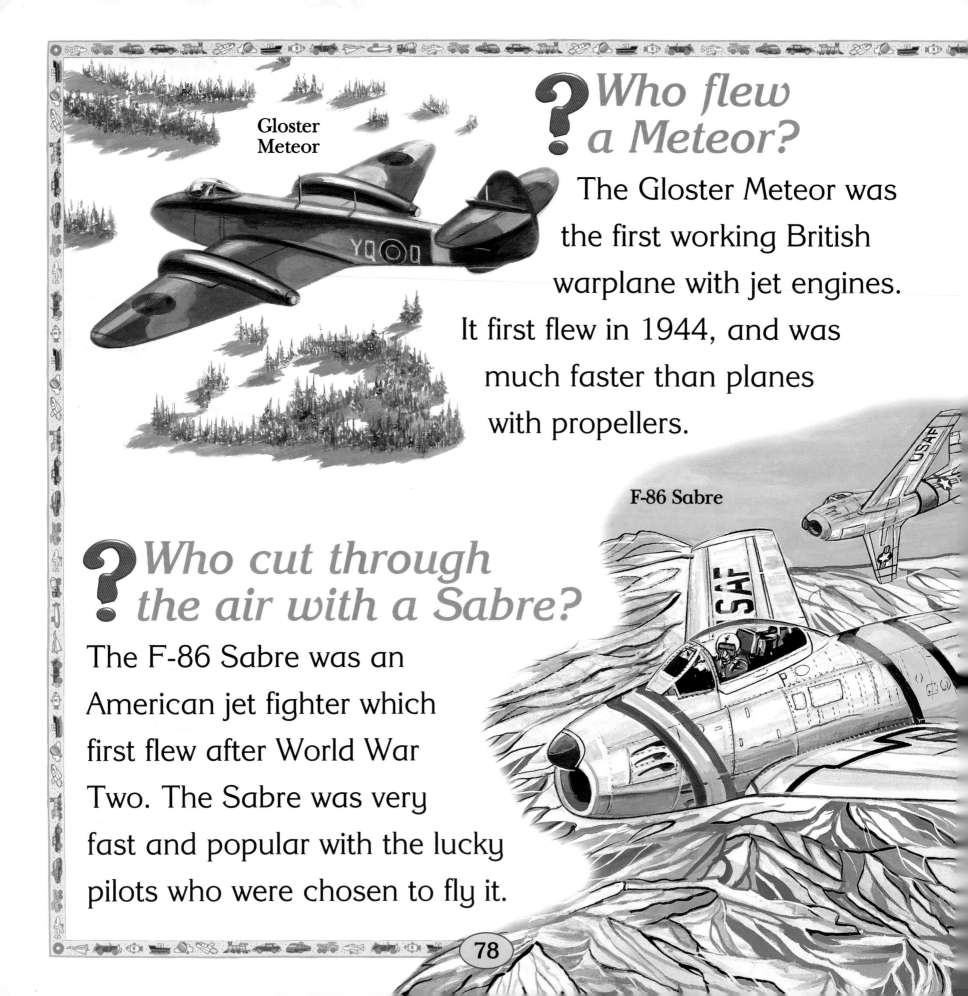

Gloster
Meteor

? Who flew a Meteor?

The Gloster Meteor was the first working British warplane with jet engines. It first flew in 1944, and was much faster than planes with propellers.

F-86 Sabre

? Who cut through the air with a Sabre?

The F-86 Sabre was an American jet fighter which first flew after World War Two. The Sabre was very fast and popular with the lucky pilots who were chosen to fly it.

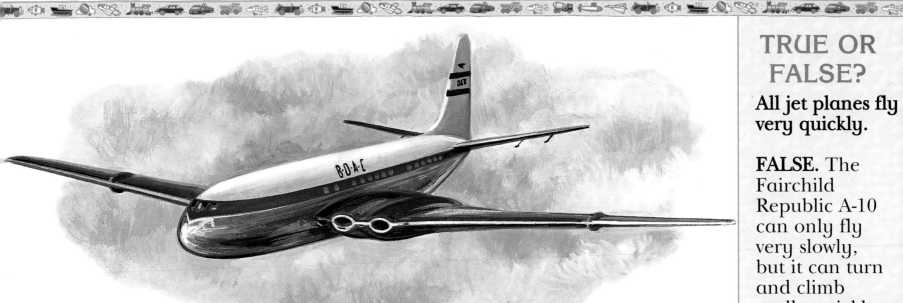

de Havilland Comet

All jet planes fly very quickly.

FALSE. The Fairchild Republic A-10 can only fly very slowly, but it can turn and climb really quickly.

? *What was a Comet?*

The de Havilland Comet was the first jet airliner to carry passengers. It had four jet engines set into its wings, and started flying between England and South Africa in 1952.

One plane had eight jet engines.

TRUE. The Boeing B-52 Stratofortress was so big, and flew so far, that it needed eight jet engines to keep it in the air!

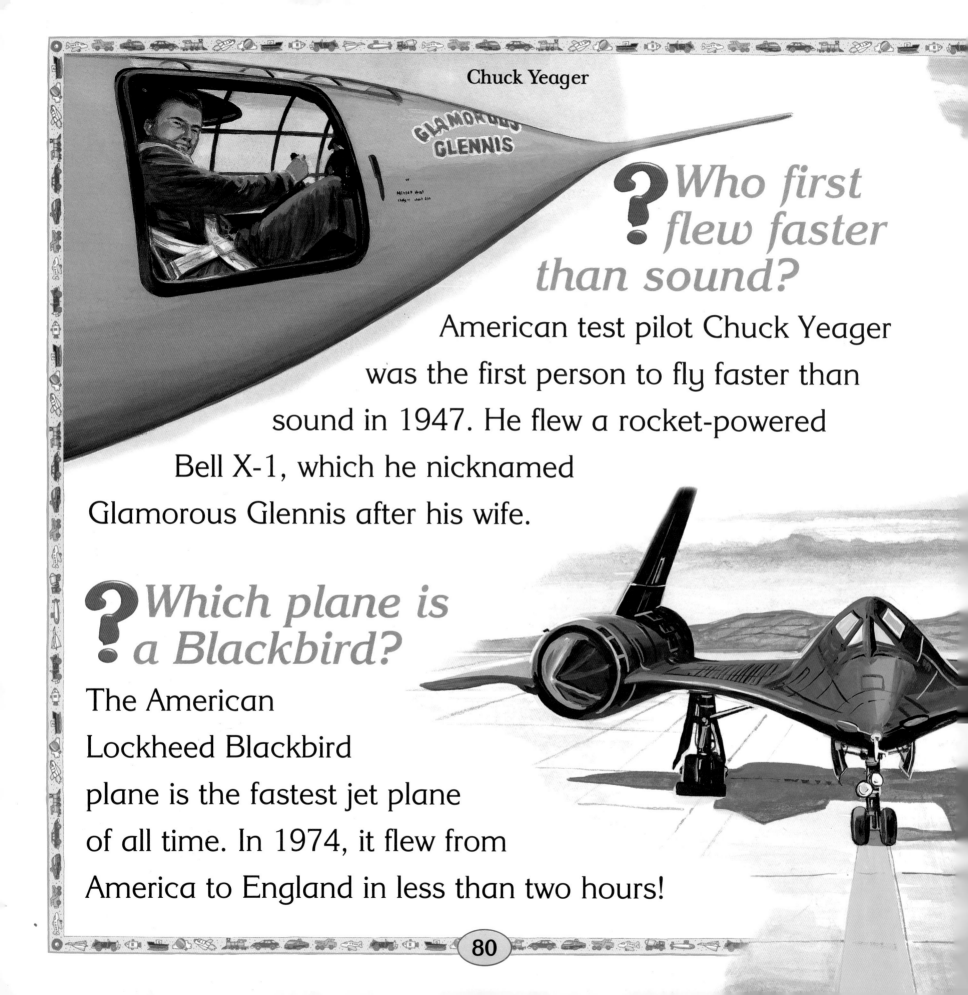

Chuck Yeager

? Who first flew faster than sound?

American test pilot Chuck Yeager was the first person to fly faster than sound in 1947. He flew a rocket-powered Bell X-1, which he nicknamed Glamorous Glennis after his wife.

? Which plane is a Blackbird?

The American Lockheed Blackbird plane is the fastest jet plane of all time. In 1974, it flew from America to England in less than two hours!

X-15 rocket plane

Blackbird

❓ *What is a rocket plane?*

Rocket planes have powerful rocket engines, which make them even faster than jet planes. The X-15 rocket plane is the fastest plane ever. It has also flown the highest – nearly 355,000 feet above the ground.

What is a delta wing?

Most planes have slim and straight wings, but some very fast planes, such as the Saab Draken and Concorde, have much larger delta wings, which are shaped like a triangle, and help the plane to travel through the air quickly.

Saab J 35F Draken

01

X-24B rocket plane

Which plane had no wings?

The X-24B had no wings. Instead, this rocket plane had a specially shaped body which helped lift the plane and keep it in the air. Only very skilled pilots could fly wingless planes.

? *Which plane has back-to-front wings?*

The Grumman X-29A has wings which face forward, so that the plane can turn sharp corners when it's traveling very quickly. The plane is difficult to control, and it can only be flown with the help of computers.

Grumman X-29A

TRUE OR FALSE?

Some planes can swing their wings.

TRUE. The Panavia Tornado swings its wings forward to take off and land, and swings them back again to fly at high speeds.

Triplanes have two wings.

FALSE. Triplanes have three sets of wings. The most famous triplane was the Red Baron's Dr I, flown in World War One.

? What is a stunt plane?

Stunt planes are usually small, agile aircraft, flown by very brave and skillful pilots. They thrill crowds by flying in groups, performing stunts, such as loops and rolls, and flying very close to the ground.

? Are there plane races?

There have been plane races almost since planes were invented. The most famous racers were the Gee Bees. These short, fat planes flew in America during the 1930s in races that were 5,000 miles long.

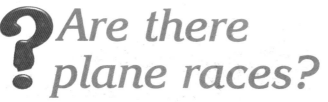

Gee Bee
racing planes

? *Where can I see stunt planes?*

Air shows take place all over the world, where you can see planes of all shapes and sizes, including stunt display teams. Why not find out if there's an air show near you?

Stunt planes

TRUE OR FALSE?

Planes can't fly upside down.

FALSE. Stunt planes often fly upside down. But pilots have to make sure that they're safely strapped in, to stop them falling out!

People can stand on planes' wings.

TRUE. "Wing walkers" have to be tightly strapped on to the wing, and wrapped up in several layers of warm clothing!

? How far can airliners travel?

Airliners can fly to the other side of the world in about 22 hours. They have to stop to fill up with fuel during the journey.

Boeing 747
"Jumbo Jet"

? What is the fastest airliner?

The fastest ever airliner is Concorde, which can travel at over twice the speed of sound. Concorde has made the trip between Europe and America in under three hours.

Concorde

Dash-7

? Can planes land in cities?

Small, quiet planes, such as the Dash-7, only need a short runway to take off and land. They are the ideal aircraft for small airports in crowded cities.

Which type of aircraft hovers?

Unlike aircraft with fixed wings, helicopters have wings called rotors, which spin around very quickly to lift them off the ground. Helicopters can also hover (stay still in the air without moving forward or backward).

Westland Sea King

What is an air ambulance?

Helicopters are often used as ambulances. They can land easily in cities, on streets or in parks, and they can take sick or injured people to hospital more quickly than a road ambulance.

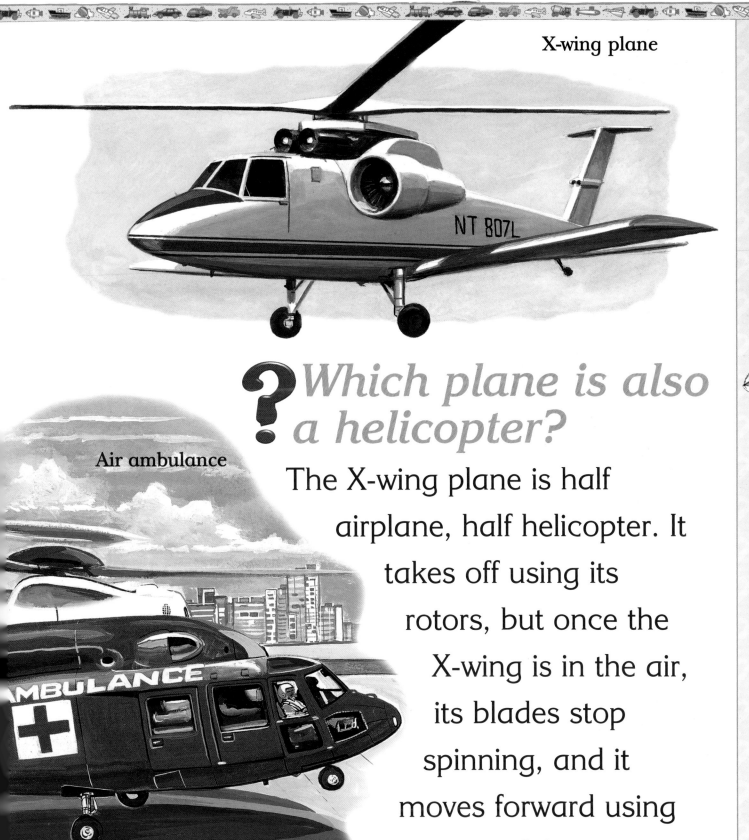

X-wing plane

Air ambulance

? *Which plane is also a helicopter?*

The X-wing plane is half airplane, half helicopter. It takes off using its rotors, but once the X-wing is in the air, its blades stop spinning, and it moves forward using two powerful jet engines.

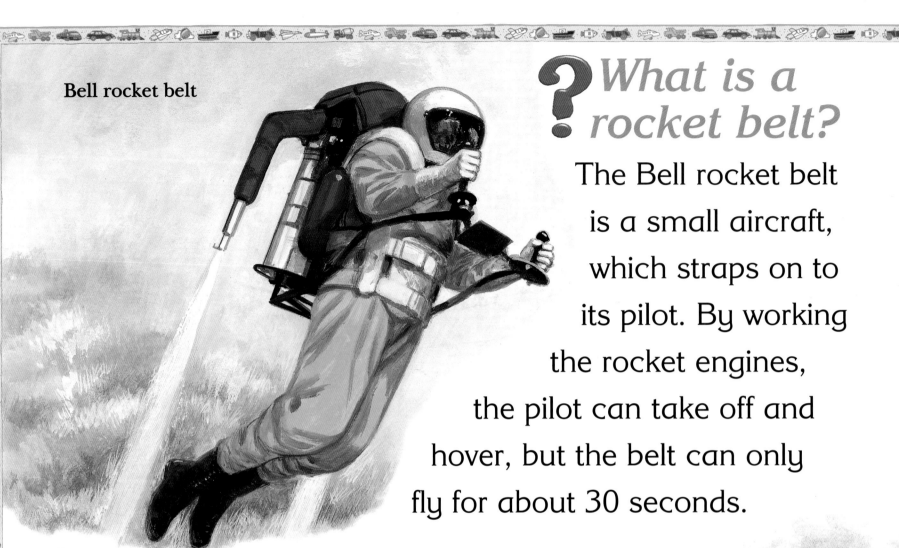

Bell rocket belt

❓ What is a rocket belt?

The Bell rocket belt is a small aircraft, which straps on to its pilot. By working the rocket engines, the pilot can take off and hover, but the belt can only fly for about 30 seconds.

❓ What is a jump-jet?

Some aircraft, such as the Harrier jump-jet, can take off straight up into the air without the need for a runway. They can also hover in the air.

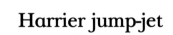

Harrier jump-jet

Osprey

? *Which plane can swivel its engines?*

The Osprey can swivel its propeller-driven engines, so that it can take off like a helicopter. Then the engines tilt forward, and it flies like an ordinary plane.

TRUE OR FALSE?

You can fly on a bed.

FALSE. But one early plane, which could take off like a jump-jet, looked so much like a bed that it was nicknamed the Flying Bedstead.

Planes have ejector seats.

TRUE. If they are in danger, the pilots of some military planes can press a button and shoot straight out of the cockpit!

What is a hang glider?

A hang glider is a very light aircraft with no engine. The pilot hangs in a harness under the wing, and steers the hang glider with a control bar.

Microlight

What is a microlight?

Microlights are tiny aircraft powered by a small engine. The pilot sits in an open cockpit under the wing, and steers the plane by moving the wing.

Hang glider

Paraglider

? *What is a paraglider?*

Paragliders look like parachutes. Sometimes pilots have a strap-on engine, or they're towed behind speed boats. As it moves along, the paraglider fills with air, and lifts its pilot up into the sky.

Super-jumbo

❓ What will airliners look like in the future?

There are plans to build new super-jumbo jets, with over 600 seats. These triple-decker planes might solve the problem of the skies becoming overcrowded with air traffic.

❓ Which plane travels in space?

The space shuttle is launched using huge rockets, which fall away as it reaches space. It has rocket engines of its own, to steer, speed up and slow down in space.

Space shuttle orbiter

?Which airliner might go into space?

One day, space planes might be able to fly passengers far above the Earth at amazing speeds. A trip between Europe and America in a space plane would only take half an hour!

Enterprise

TRUE OR FALSE?

The shuttle is a glider.

TRUE. The space shuttle's engines run out of fuel in space. When the shuttle returns to Earth, it floats down as a glider.

The shuttle is covered in tiles.

TRUE. The shuttle gets very hot when it returns to Earth. It has thousands of special tiles which protect it from the heat.

What is the shuttle used for?

and other questions about spacecraft

❓Who invented the first rockets?

Small firework-like rockets were invented in China about 1,000 years ago. The Chinese used to fire them at their enemies during battles.

❓Which rocket first used liquid fuel?

Robert Goddard launched the first liquid-fueled rocket in 1926. His rocket only went 13 yards into the air (about as high as seven people), and landed 70 yards away. All spacecraft are launched using liquid fuel rockets.

Robert Goddard

? *Why do spacecraft need rockets?*

Jet engines and gasoline engines need air to work. They would be no use in space, because there's no air in space. Rocket engines don't need air, so they can work just as well in space as they do on Earth.

Ariane rocket

? What is a satellite?

A satellite is any object which orbits (travels around) the Earth. The Earth's natural satellite is the Moon. The first man-made satellite was Sputnik 1, which was launched in 1957.

Sputnik 1

? How do satellites use the Sun?

Satellites can carry on working for a long time because the Sun gives them energy. Satellites have solar panels, like wings, which soak up light and heat from the Sun, and turn them into electricity.

Solar panels

❓ *What do satellites do?*

Satellites do lots of jobs. Some of them take pictures of Earth to tell us about the weather, and some are used for spying on other countries. Communications satellites bounce television and telephone signals back to Earth.

Telstar communications satellite

❓ Who was the first astronaut?

The first earthling in space wasn't a person – it was a Russian dog called Laika. She spent seven days orbiting the Earth aboard a small spacecraft called Sputnik 2 in 1957. Laika's journey proved that space flight would be safe for humans.

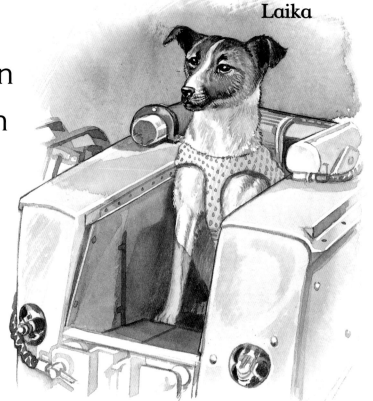

Laika

❓ Who was the first person in space?

Russian pilot Yuri Gagarin became the first person in space in 1961. He orbited the Earth once in a Vostok 1 spacecraft. His journey only took an hour and a half. He was given a hero's welcome when he returned to Earth.

Yuri Gagarin

? *Who went back to space after 36 years?*

John Glenn became the first American to orbit the Earth in 1962, when he was 41 years old. 36 years later, he went back, and became the oldest ever astronaut. He carried out experiments to see if space travel was more dangerous for older people.

John Glenn

? Why do astronauts need space suits?

Space suits protect astronauts from the extreme heat and cold of space, and from dangerous radiation. They also give astronauts air to breathe, and stop their bodies from exploding!

? How do astronauts repair satellites?

Astronauts repair satellites using the smallest of all manned spacecraft – the Manned Maneuvering Unit (MMU). The astronaut straps on the MMU, and flies through space, using 24 small jets of gas.

MMU in action

? Why do things float around in space?

You don't float around here on Earth, because gravity is always pulling you toward the Earth's surface. In outer space, far away from other worlds, there's no gravity, so everything floats around, including astronauts!

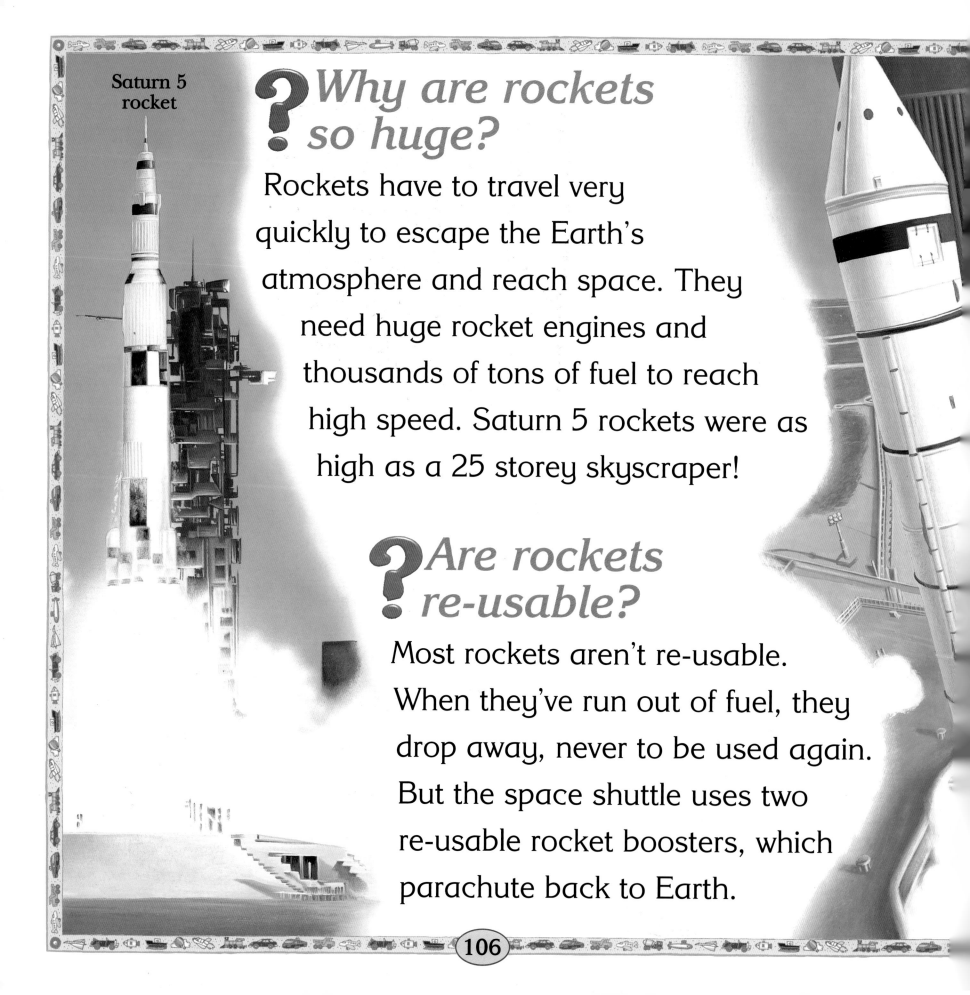

Saturn 5 rocket

? Why are rockets so huge?

Rockets have to travel very quickly to escape the Earth's atmosphere and reach space. They need huge rocket engines and thousands of tons of fuel to reach high speed. Saturn 5 rockets were as high as a 25 storey skyscraper!

? Are rockets re-usable?

Most rockets aren't re-usable. When they've run out of fuel, they drop away, never to be used again. But the space shuttle uses two re-usable rocket boosters, which parachute back to Earth.

Shuttle launch

❓ *Are rockets all in one piece?*

Rockets are made up of several pieces, or stages. The lower stages contain fuel and rocket engines. When they run out of fuel, they're no longer needed. So each empty stage drops away, one by one.

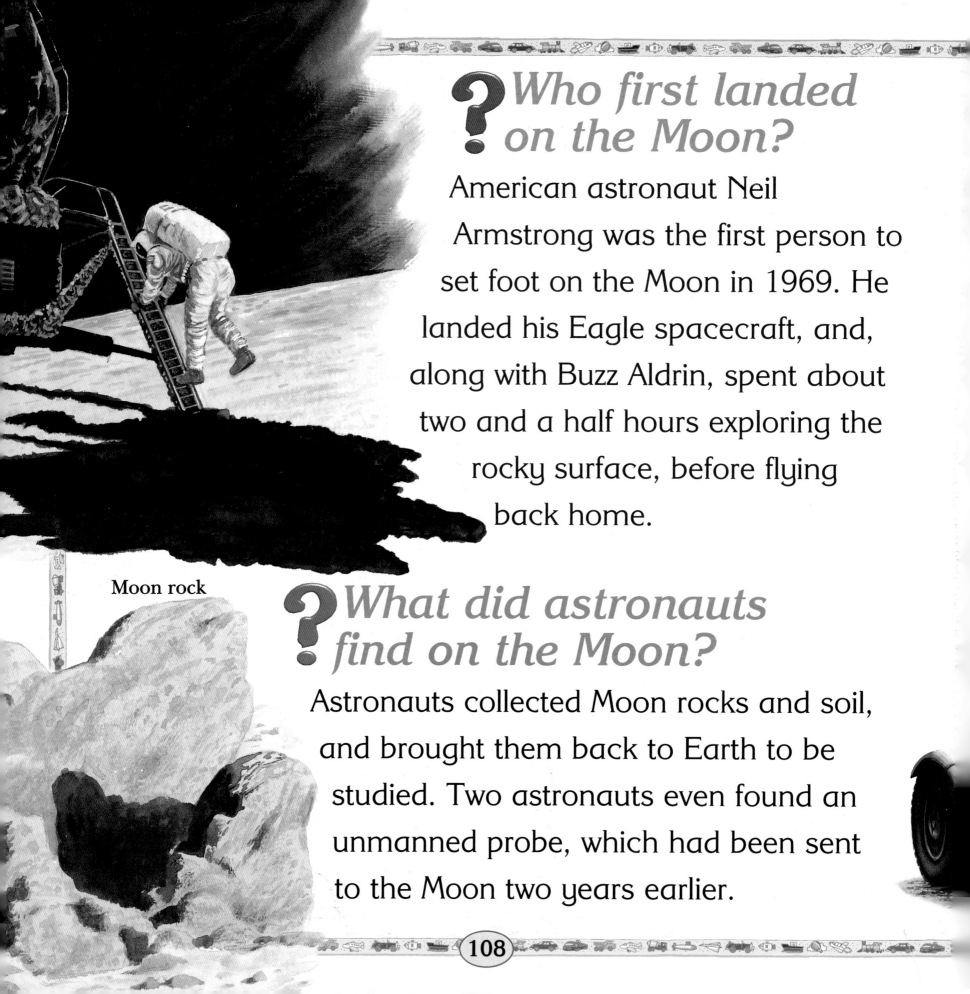

Who first landed on the Moon?

American astronaut Neil Armstrong was the first person to set foot on the Moon in 1969. He landed his Eagle spacecraft, and, along with Buzz Aldrin, spent about two and a half hours exploring the rocky surface, before flying back home.

Moon rock

What did astronauts find on the Moon?

Astronauts collected Moon rocks and soil, and brought them back to Earth to be studied. Two astronauts even found an unmanned probe, which had been sent to the Moon two years earlier.

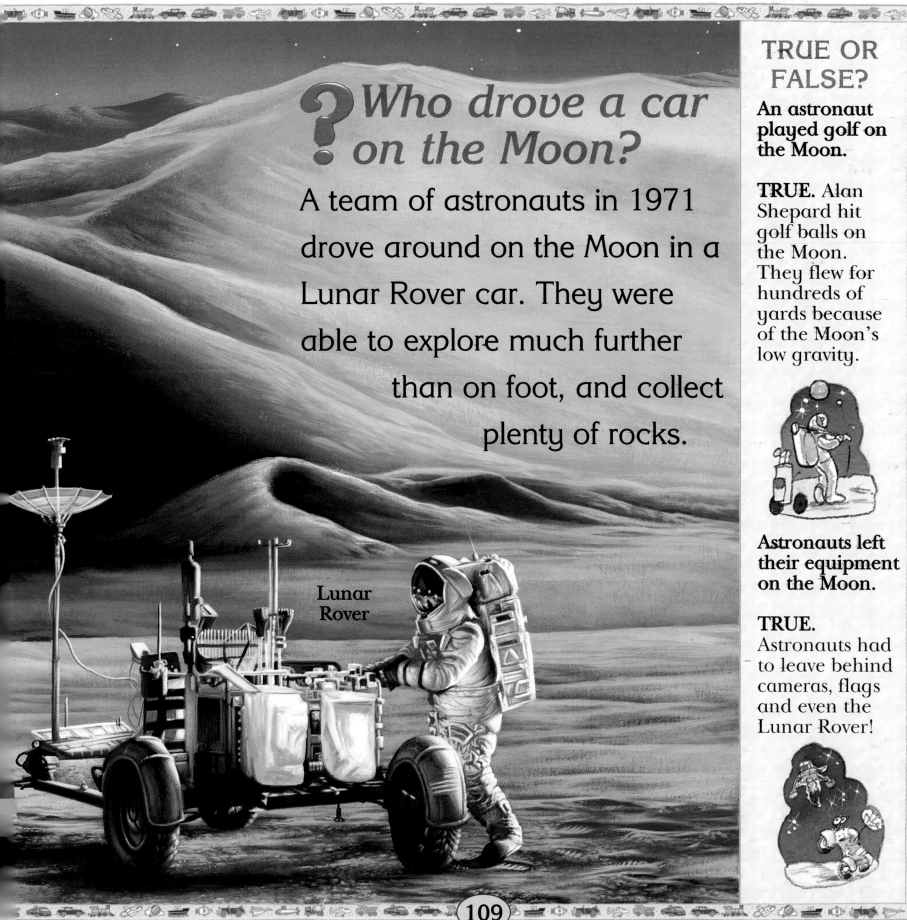

? Who drove a car on the Moon?

A team of astronauts in 1971 drove around on the Moon in a Lunar Rover car. They were able to explore much further than on foot, and collect plenty of rocks.

Lunar Rover

Apollo 13

? Who didn't make it to the Moon?

There was an explosion aboard the Apollo 13 spacecraft, during a trip to the Moon. The crew were ordered to return to Earth. They only just made it home before they ran out of air.

? What can you see from the Moon?

The sky over the Moon is always black. The Earth seems very large and bright, as it rises and sets over the horizon. You can also see the Sun and the stars.

?How long did it take to reach the Moon?

Our nearest neighbor, the Moon, is about 238,000 miles from the Earth. Even with the help of fast and powerful rockets, astronauts had to sit in their spacecraft for four and a half days before they reached the Moon.

TRUE OR FALSE?

The Moon is covered in water.

FALSE. The Moon has several "seas" but they're full of rocks and dust, not water. But scientists think there might be frozen water at the Moon's poles.

Russian astronauts have visited the Moon.

FALSE. Twelve astronauts have walked on the Moon – all of them were American.

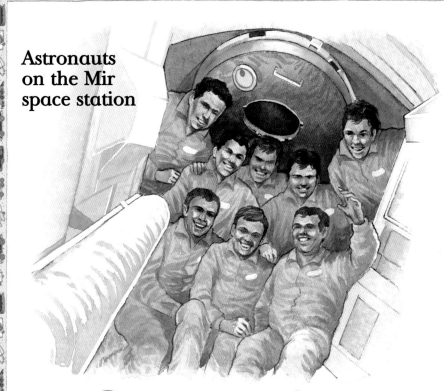

Astronauts on the Mir space station

?How do you eat in space?

Astronauts take dried food into space. They add water, to turn it into a proper meal. You have to eat carefully in space, in case your food floats off the plate!

?Can people live in space?

People have stayed in space stations for over a year, but space travel can be bad for your health. Astronauts' bones, hearts and muscles become weak unless they take plenty of exercise.

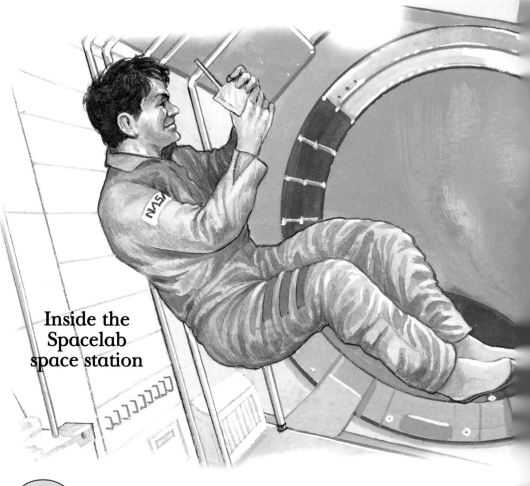

Inside the Spacelab space station

?*What happens when space stations close down?*

Once space stations are abandoned, they usually fall back to Earth, and burn up in the atmosphere. But the American Skylab space station didn't burn up, and parts of it fell on to farmland in Australia.

Skylab burning up

Which spacecraft can be used again?

Space shuttle

Early spacecraft could only be used once, but the American space shuttle and the Russian Buran spaceplane were designed to be used many times. Six space shuttles have been built. Between them, they have made over 100 space flights.

What is the shuttle used for?

Early shuttle missions carried large satellites into space. But after the shuttle Challenger exploded in 1986, scientists thought it would be safer to use unmanned rockets to launch satellites. These days, the shuttle is used for satellite repair, building a space station and finding out more about space.

❓ *What is a robot arm?*

The shuttle has a 41 foot-long arm, which is used to grab satellites and other objects in space, and put them into the shuttle. Just like your arms, it has shoulder, elbow and wrist joints. Astronauts can even hitch a ride on the arm!

Robot arm

? Who landed in the sea?

Astronauts on all the early American space missions parachuted into the sea in their capsules. Navy ships or helicopters kept in touch with the astronauts, collected them, and took them safely back to shore.

? What is mission control?

Mission control is the name for the team of scientists and space experts on Earth, who control every space mission. Mission control talks to astronauts by radio, giving them orders and helping out in emergencies.

Mission control

? *How do spacecraft return to Earth?*

Spacecraft get very hot when they enter the Earth's atmosphere. The shuttle is covered in heat-proof tiles to protect it. It lands on a runway, just like a normal airplane.

Shuttle returning to Earth

TRUE OR FALSE?

Yuri Gagarin parachuted back to Earth.

TRUE. Yuri Gagarin ejected from his space capsule and floated to the ground using a parachute.

The shuttle is a glider.

TRUE. The shuttle glides back to the ground. This is because it has run out of fuel.

What used balloons to land on Mars?

The Pathfinder probe parachuted on to Mars inside some balloons. When the balloons deflated, a robot car called Sojourner drove away over them.

Pathfinder probe

What is a space probe?

Voyager probe

A space probe is an unmanned spacecraft, which sends pictures of other planets and their moons back to Earth. Some probes, such as Pathfinder, land on other planets. The Voyager probes flew past the planets, and are now heading toward the stars.

Giotto probe

Probes get lost in space.

TRUE. Several Mars probes exploded, crashed or missed the planet. Some probes simply went missing.

Pioneer carries a message.

TRUE. Pioneer carries a map of where it came from, and a picture of a man and a woman. Maybe aliens will find it and visit us!

? *Which probe chased a comet?*

The Giotto probe chased Halley's comet when it passed Earth in 1986. Giotto proved that the comet was a large, dirty snowball, orbiting the Sun. To protect it from the comet's long, dusty tail, Giotto had a special shield.

Is there a space telescope?

The Hubble space telescope was launched by a space shuttle in 1990. On Earth, the view of the stars is often spoilt by pollution and street lights. In space, Hubble doesn't have these problems, so it sends us amazing pictures.

Hubble space
telescope

Eagle Nebula

❓ *What can Hubble see?*

The Hubble space telescope can see a very long way into space. It has taken pictures of the Eagle Nebula – a massive cloud of gas. Inside the fingers of cloud, the gas is gathering together to make new stars. Hubble is so sensitive, it could spot a coin 400 miles away!

TRUE OR FALSE?

Hubble needed to wear glasses.

TRUE. Hubble couldn't see very well at first. Astronauts gave it new lenses, which work like glasses, and it can see much better now.

Hubble has seen alien spacecraft.

FALSE. Hubble has taken pictures of stars in distant parts of the Universe, but it hasn't found any sign of alien life.

? *What will spacecraft look like in the future?*

The space shuttle is very expensive to launch. American scientists think that the VentureStar space plane might be cheaper. VentureStar could be used to launch other spacecraft in orbit.

VentureStar

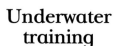

Underwater training

? *How can I become an astronaut?*

You have to train for several years to become an astronaut. Here on Earth, astronauts practice space-walking in water tanks. This gives them an idea of how floating in space will feel.

? *Will there be cities in space?*

One day, spacecraft might be used to build cities or even hotels in space. Once the International Space Station has been built, it will be a permanent home for astronauts.

International Space Station

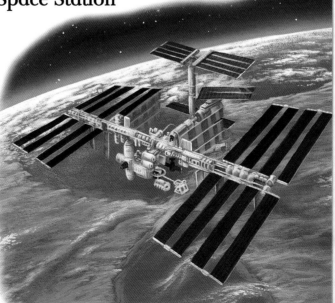

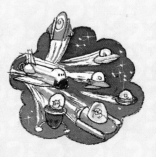

? Is there life on other planets?

Scientists are sure there isn't life on any planet near Earth. But there might be on one of Saturn's moons – Titan. The Huygens probe will parachute on to Titan in 2004 to look for any signs of life.

Huygens probe

? Will people ever live on other planets?

It might be possible for robots to build airtight buildings on Mars. People could live inside, and grow plants, which would make air and water. Gradually people would be able to live anywhere on the planet.

Mars base of the future

? *Will we ever travel to other stars?*

If a space rocket was sent to the nearest star to our Sun, the journey would last over 150,000 years. We will probably never travel to other stars.

Spacecraft of the future

TRUE OR FALSE?

Scientists discovered Martian life.

FALSE. But scientists once thought, wrongly, that some crystals inside a rock from Mars were fossils.

There are very tall volcanoes on Mars.

TRUE. The biggest volcano on Mars is 15 miles high – nearly three times higher than Mount Everest, Earth's highest peak.

Index

electric cars 13, 25, 35

Eole 10

F-86 Sabre 78

fire trucks 60, 61, 63

Flyer 70

flying boats 76, 77

Ford Model "T" 14

Ford Mustang 27

forklift trucks 54

Formula One 20

freezer trucks 56

Gagarin, Yuri 102, 117

garbage trucks 58

Gee Bees 84

Glenn, John 103

gliders 69, 95

Gloster Meteor 78

Goddard, Robert 98

Grumman X-29A 83

hang-gliders 92

Harrier jump-jet 90

helicopters 88, 89

hot rods 29

Hubble 120, 121

Indycars 21

jackknife 46

Jamais Contente 13

KITT 33

Laika 102

limousines 22

loggers 54

Lotus Esprit 28

low-loader 44

Lunar Rover 109

microlights 92, 93

MMU 104

mobile crane 65

mobile hospitals 60

monster trucks 49

Moon landings 108-111

Osprey 91

paragliders 93

Paris-Dakar rally 62

pickups 49, 63